The Road by Heart

Poems of Fatherhood

The Road by Heart

Poems of Fatherhood

edited by

Greg Watson and
Richard Broderick

NODIN PRESS

A complete list of Acknowledgments begins on page 121.

ISBN:978-1-947237-09-4

Design: John Toren

Library of Congress Control Number: 2018946885

Nodin Press, LLC
5114 Cedar Lake Road
Minneapolis, MN
55416

www.nodinpress.com

For Hadley Frances. *No matter what.*

— *G. W.*

To my daughter and son, Emma and Gabriel.

— *R. B.*

CONTENTS

INTRODUCTION

Is it something one assumes, becomes, or earns?
Does it happen at conception, birth, acknowledgement, or
at the moment of choice?

Who confers it: the child, society, the other parent, oneself?

Once begun, does it continue? Is it temporary? Does it
come and go?
Can one be more of, yes, even less of a father?

How will I know when I become one?
Tell me how it feels. How does one prepare?

Questions, gushing from deep inside as
Boys becoming men add to their role collection
A role so awesome the strongest can cringe in fright
And for which the weakest muster and discover courage
never felt before

Fatherhood: whether birth, step, gay, adoptive, grand or
        foster
Can when assumed, chose or acknowledged,
Not to mention if earned or conferred,
Become the most humbling, curious, unpredictable,
exciting, warm, demanding giving, liberating
Experience known to man

In the pages that follow, fathers offer their own accounts about being fathers. This is a volume by fathers about being a father. There are numerous books about parenting and family development. There is few if any books like this one. Greg Watson and Richard Broderick have masterfully gathered poignant, first-hand accounts of moments in a father's life, from teething to burying; reflective poems describing the arc of fatherhood; accounts of insight, struggle, grief and delight gained while being a father; epiphanies that only occur to parents; and poems that you will carry with you long after you put this book down.

As a father, stepfather and grandfather, I have yearned for this book. I am delighted to introduce this volume. My sons, grandsons and many others will be enriched in conversations with these poet fathers!

– Ted Bowman, long-time family and grief educator

ONE

"Children bring with them grace, patience, transcendence, second chances, rebirth, and a reawakening of the love that's in your heart and present in your home. They are God giving you another shot."

— Bruce Springsteen

TO MAKE A BABY

James P. Lenfestey

These days, it takes courage.

No one has enough money.
No one has enough time.
No way is there enough room
in the house.

So you find yourself crowded
into that double bed.
And the kids are asleep.
And the checkbook is downstairs.
And you bump into something warm.

And you find your courage rising.

CONIFEROUS FATHERS

Michael Kleber-Diggs

Let's fashion gentle fathers, expressive – holding us
how we wanted to be held before we could ask.

Singing off-key lullabies, written for us – songs
every evening, like possibilities.

Fathers who say, "this is how you hold a baby"
but never mention a football.

Who say nothing in that moment, who just bring us
to their chests naturally, without shyness.

Let's grow fathers from pine, not oak, coniferous fathers
raising us in their shade, fathers soft enough to bend –

fathers who love us like their fathers couldn't.
Fathers who can talk about menstruation

while playing a game of pepper in the front yard.
No, take baseball out. Let's discover a new sort –

fathers as varied and vast as the Superior forest.
Let's kill off sternness and downplay wisdom;

give us fathers of laughter and fathers who cry,
fathers who say *check this out* and *I don't know*

or *I'm scared* or *I'm sorry.* Give us fathers
strong enough to admit they want to be near us,

they've always wanted to be near us.
Give us fathers desperate for something different,

not Johnny Appleseeds, not even Atticus Finch.
No more rolling stones. No more La-Z-Boy dads

reading the newspapers in some other room.
Let's create folklore side-by-side in a garden

Singing psalms about abiding – just that – abiding:
being steadfast, present, evergreen and ethereal –

let's make the old needles soft enough for us to rest on,
dream on – dreams of peace, at peace,

next to them, next to them.

HELLO

Sean Hill

She, being the midwife
and your mother's
longtime friend, said
I see a heart; can you
see it? And on the grey
display of the ultrasound
there you were as you were,
our nugget, in that moment
becoming a shrimp
or a comma punctuating
the whole of my life, separating
its parts - before and after -,
a shrimp in the sea
of your mother, and I couldn't
help but see the fast
beating of your heart
translated on that screen
and think and say to her,
to the room, to your mother,
to myself *It looks like*
a twinkling star.
I imagine I'm not
the first to say that either.
But unlike the first moments
of my every day which is every
moment after this one,
the new of seeing you was *the* first
-Deserving of the definite article-
moment I saw a star
at once so small and so
big, so close and getting closer
every day, I pray.

PERHAPS YOU WERE NEVER SO SMALL

GREG WATSON

for my daughter

Perhaps you were never as small
as our simple eyes
observed, but merely
coming from a distance
we could not measure,
a star whose light had traveled
centuries before
it could be seen or named.
Perhaps this is the point where
time itself slows
to an audible pulse,
one clenched hand conducting
through the bone-lit dark,
the thick rhythm of
our steps leading
continuously home,
through the shadowless
shift of moon
and vapor trails of memory,
leaning back
into a music that
could only be learned by heart,
a music that was somehow
made for us all along,
long before we had bodies
and mouths with which to sing.

I KNEW YOU BEFORE YOU WERE

Alex Lemon

Rusty chains coiled in the cardboard box
      I carry to the dumpster & all I am

Thinking this is my face is falling off & is yours
      Under it & or is someone's I don't

Even know – further down, a stranger,
      A deadman, a saint, or just a sprawl

Of gravel & then I'm thinking this other thing –
      There's a snake in this box, blacktailed

& then more: there's a bottomless immensity
      Beneath my feet & what a sacrifice

It is each day just to get by, this alchemy,
      This fevered life: illness & love,

Lockjaw & slow motion kidnappings – It is what
      It always is – chronic dying, shivering with

Unbelievable joy & not knowing a damn thing
      About anything as lightning

Jigsaws at the horizon. At the garbage pile, I pause –
      Take a deep breath & sit on the curb.

Like they're being sucked into the sky,
      The trees' limbs lift. No cars on

The street – so quiet. So hushed I can
　　Hardly breathe. Thousands of lives

Are piled into all this dirt we walk
　　On & I'm waiting, saving it all for you.

ON THE DAY MY DAUGHTER WAS BORN NO ONE DIED

Yehuda Amichai

translated by Chana Bloch and Stephen Mitchell

On the day my daughter was born no one died
In the hospital and at the entrance
Was written: "today the *Cohanim* may enter."
Out of great joy
I went with my friend to the hills of Sha'ar Hagay.

We saw a sick, bare pine tree covered only with countless
pine cones. Zvi said that tress about to die bear more cones
than the vital ones. I said to him: That was a poem and you
didn't even realize it. Even though you are a man of exact
sciences you made a poem. He replied: and even though
you are a man of dreams, you made a precise little girl with
all the precise instruments for her life.

IN THE NEWBORN INTENSIVE CARE UNIT

GREG WATSON

It is best to speak softly here, to make
only the smallest of conversation with those
in passing; a weary nod in the elevator
is easily understood, acknowledgement of the obvious
and hope for transcendence, however fleeting.
From our cool and colorless room we stand watch,
our tiny daughter breathing in a time signature
we cannot follow, though it surrounds us,
along with our seeming helplessness, learning
what new words and phrases we can – the jargon
of those who know which wire goes where,
which numbers are good news, and which
elicit only a slightly somber exhalation.
A gentle and unexpected humor rises between
us, born of a weary necessity. Saltines, and tumblers
of chipped ice from the machine down the hall
become an almost religious ritual, though
we pass the small, silent chapel with its huddled
congregation of candles glowing at all hours.
Mostly we wait with the others, sleeping
sporadically on fold-out cots, never sure which
bleeps from the machines signal safety,
and which a possible storm just out of view.

WHAT EFFECT HAS YOUR NEW SON HAD ON YOUR WRITING LIFE?

RICHARD JONES

While Andrew sleeps
in the room that used to be my study
I go downstairs to a desk
in a corner of the basement
to write. And each day when he wakes
I sit him in my lap and keep working,
bouncing him on my knee and typing
like I used to, quickly with one finger,
reciting lines to see
if my poems put him to sleep.
That's heaven – writing poetry,
Andrew in my arms. Though I abandon
the most divinely inspired poem when
Andrew wants his bottle.

ON THE BIRTH OF A SON

SU TUNG-PO

translated by Arthur Waley

Families when a child is born
Hope it will turn out intelligent.
I, through intelligence
Having wrecked my whole life,
Only hope that the baby will prove
Ignorant and stupid.
Then he'll be happy all his days
And grow into a cabinet minister.

GARY YOUNG

It's a joy to be subtracted from the world. Holding my son's naked body against my own, all I feel is what he is. I cannot feel my own skin. I cannot feel myself touching him, but I can recognize his hair, the heft of his body, his warmth, his weight. I cannot measure my own being, my subtle boundaries, but I know my son's arms, the drape of his legs, smooth and warm in a shape I can measure. I have become such a fine thing, the resting-place for a body I can know.

TEETHING

KEVIN YOUNG

Wisdom and love have nothing to do with each other.
Wisdom is staying alive, survival. You're wise if you don't
stick your finger in the light plug. Love – you'll stick your
finger in anything.

            – Robert Altman

The mouth is the most
potent instrument an infant
possess – no wonder

you put your tongue
to anything, or anything
in your mouth. Roots

of teeth teasing just below
your gums. Drool
is your muse,

your song or cry
always full. Unlike us,
you love being

changed. It is only
sleep you mind – missing
the world's noise, what wisdom

the widows know. The bell
of your mouth ringing
in morning.

ALREADY WAVING

Chad Prevost

At eighteen months my son has waved goodbye
some thousand times it seems.
It's safe to say he is always pumping,
or preparing to pump, his fingers & wrists.

He waves goodbye to the grass & ducks
as he steps through the door inside,
to his crib when he wakes from a nap.
He waves to the grocery carts

pushed by his adoring fans – mothers
cooing & babbling baby talk.
He sucks his pacifier as if in thought, waving –
waving as he does when he runs

from the bee that buzzes in his face
by the backyard flowers. By evening,
he has waved away swings & slides,
even his peas that dot the floor after dinner

as his mother sweeps him away for a bath,
where soon he'll wave to the draining water,
the rubber turtle, his tugboat swirling,
&, finally, to his mother's bedtime song.

If it weren't for the way he slams his fists
to the floor & kicks the air
when he wants juice, & wails when he wants out
I might mistake his waving for wisdom,

imagine he sees into the core of some simple
yet elusive truth, not the inevitable one
that the world doesn't revolve around him,
but that even now we're already waving goodbye.

FIRST LESSON

Philip Booth

Lie back, daughter, let your head
be tipped back in the cup of my hand.
Gently, and I will hold you. Spread
your arms wide, lie out on the stream
and look high at the gulls. A dead-
man's-float is face down. You will dive
and swim soon enough where this tidewater
ebbs to the sea. Daughter, believe
me, when you tire on the long thrash
to your island, lie up, and survive.
As you float now, where I held you
and let go, remember when fear
cramps your heart what I told you:
lie gently and wide to the light-year
stars, lie back, and the sea will hold you.

The baby fusses. I read a book to quiet him, and he calms. His fingers open, show a lifeline, heartline, all the fates lurking in his flesh. He's asleep when I finish, and one hand closes in a fist around my thumb. Somewhere he's learned even dreams must be tethered to the earth.

FACES

STEPHEN DOBYNS

My daughter baby Clio lies on her back
on the sheepskin rug, jerking her arms and feet
like a turtle stuck upside down in the dirt
struggling to get out. But here there is no threat,
I tell myself. The room is benign and I
act for the best. She is just contentedly
wriggling. It is nothing like a turtle flipped
over while two or three crows sidle closer,
eager to pluck her soft parts. The room is safe
and I direct my life to keep it like that.
How much of this is fiction I believe in?
We are forced to live in a place without walls
and I build her shelter with bits of paper.
The ever-attentive beaks surround us. These
birds are her future – face of a teacher, face
of a thief, one with the face of her father.

TWO

I have daughters and I have sons.
When one of them lays a hand
on my shoulder, shining fish
turn suddenly in the deep sea.

— Robert Bly

FATHER, CHILD, WATER

Gary Dop

I lift your body to the boat
before you drown or choke or slip too far

beneath. I didn't' think—just jumped, just did
what I did like the physics

that flung you in. My hands clutch under
year-old arms, between your life

jacket and your bobbing frame, pushing you,
like a fountain cherub, up and out.

I'm fooled by the warmth pulsing from
the gash on my thigh, sliced wide and clean

by an errant screw on the stern.
No pain. My legs kick out blood below.

My arms strain
against our deaths to hold you up

as I lift you, crying, reaching, to the boat.

marina:

CHARLES BUKOWSKI

majestic, magic
infinite
my little girl is
sun
on the carpet –
out the door
picking a
flower, ha!,
an old man,
battle-wrecked,
emerges from his
chair
and she looks at me
but only sees
love,
ha!, and I become
quick with the world
and love right back
just like I was meant
to do.

SHE KNOWS THE SOUND OF ONE HAND APPLAUDING GOD'S CREATION

HARDY COLEMAN

There are places, I hear, where she'd be considered
almost normal.
Brown hair with a touch of wave,
her first training bra,
a hand on her right side,
none on the left.
There's a town in Iraq
where all the kids are missing something;
an eye, a leg, the ability to speak. . .

It's the miracle of birth:
Roll the dice and see what you get.
It is the wonder of commerce:
Buy now, pay later.
And the ease of technology:
Turn on the lights and hear the rivers scream.

The graceful children prance and tumble
learning how to compensate. hop scotch with what they got.
5, 6, 7, 8,
a clipped wing angel's curly gait.

All the fifth graders have wooden flutes
which they unwrap and blow on festival days
for the parents, the teachers, for each other.
It's a joyous occasion, and I mean that.
My daughter cannot play the flute,
but she sings in the choir like a bird of prey.
There are no repercussions for who she takes

with her one, quick talon.
Her voice is the aftershock of lightening,
wind chiming the clouds.
In its presence I can fly
and I don't need permission,
my little girl just sends me!

At the birth
in our home, in our bedroom
with my wife, with friends and siblings
I held hear steaming, creamy six pounds of body close.
Complete. Five fingers and ten toes.
I adored her then, as I do now.
But I hated God that day,
and still, I'd trade my arm for hers.

When she was three days old we took her in
and Doctor Mayer, he told me,
"It's not the maker's fault, so let him off the hook.
There could be five-hundred reasons why.
You'll never find the one."
But if I do,
and it was you. . . I love my child.
I will make you pay.

SEPTEMBER, THE FIRST DAY OF SCHOOL

Howard Nemerov

I

My child and I hold hands on the way to school,
And when I leave him at the first-grade door
He cries a little but is brave; he does
Leg go. My selfish tears remind me how
I cried before that door a life ago.
I may have had a hard time letting go.

Each fall the children must endure together
What every child also endures alone:
Learning the alphabet, the integers,
Three dozen bits and pieces of a stuff
That worlds invisible and visible

Bow down before it, as in Joseph's dream
The sheaves bowed down and then the stars bowed down
Before the dreaming of a little boy.
That dream got him such hatred of his brothers
As cost the greater part of life to mend
And yet great kindness came of it in the end.

II

A school is where they grind the grain of thought,
And grind the children who must mind the thought.
It may be those two grindings are but one,
As from the alphabet come Shakespeare's Plays,
As from the integers comes Euler's Law,
As from the whole, inseperably, the lives,

The shrunken lives that have not been set free
By law or by poetic phantasy.
But may they be. My child has disappeared
Behind the schoolroom door. And should I live
To see his coming forth, a life away,
I know my hope, but do not know its form

Nor hope to know it. May the fathers he finds
Among his teachers have a care of him
More than his father could. how that will look
I do not know, I do not need to know.
Even our tears belong to ritual.
But may great kindness come of it in the end.

EGG

C. G. HANZLICEK

I'm scrambling an egg for my daughter.
"Why are you always whistling?" she asks.
"Because I'm happy."
And it's true,
Though it stuns me to say it aloud.
There was a time when I wouldn't
Have seen it as my future.
It's partly a matter
Of who is there to eat the egg.
The self fallen out of love with itself
Through the tedium of familiarity,
Or this little self,
So curious, so hungry,
Who emerged from the woman I love,
A woman who loves me in a way
I've come to think I deserve,
Now that it arrives from outside me.
Everything changes, we're told,
And now the changes are everywhere:
The house with its morning light
That fills me like a revelation,
The yard with its trees
That cast a bit more shade each summer,
The love of a woman
That both is and isn't confounding,
And the love
Of this clamor of questions at my waist.
Clamor of questions,
Your clamor of answers,
Here's your egg.

A HAZEL STICK FOR CATHERINE ANN

Seamus Heaney

The living mother-of-pearl of a salmon
just out of the water

is gone just like that, but your stick
is kept salmon-silver.

Seasoned and bendy,
it convinces the hand

that what you have you hold
to play with and pose with

and lay about with.
But then too it points back to cattle

and spatter and beating
the bars of a gate –

the very stick we might cut
from your family tree.

The living cobalt of an afternoon
dragonfly drew my eye to it first

and the evening I trimmed it for you
you saw your first glow-worm –

all of us stood round in silence, even you
gigantic enough to darken the sky

for a glow-worm.
And when I poked open the grass

a tiny brightening den lit the eye
in the blunt pared end of your stick.

A KITE FOR MICHAEL
AND CHRISTOPHER

Seamus Heaney

All through that Sunday afternoon
a kite flew above Sunday,
a tightened drumhead, an armful of brown chaff.

I'd seen it grey and slippery in the making,
I'd tapped it when it dried out white and stiff,
I'd tied the bows of newspaper
along its six-foot tail.

But now it was far up like a small black lark
and now it dragged as if the bellied string
were a wet rope hauled upon
to lift a shoal.

My friend says that the human soul
is about the weight of a snipe,
yet the soul at anchor there,
the string that sags and ascends,
weigh like a furrow assumed into the heavens.

Before the kite plunges down into the wood
and this line goes useless
take in your two hands, boys, and feel
the strumming, rooted, long-tailed pull of grief.
You were born fit for it.
Stand in here in front of me
and take the strain.

ANDREW TALKS TO GULLS

George Roberts

for my son

standing on a string of grey rocks
reaching out into the clear water
andrew talks to gulls

his voice   sliding through octave cries
light as time   lifts in clouds of gulls
and draws their tiny black eyes

he thinks those pure white birds come
out of the sky and across years of water
for the pieces of bread he scatters to them

I know the sun dancing on their yellow beaks
is in honor of this small boy
whose voice remembers

he too once wore
white feathers

FREIGHT

By the time this rumination
    is delivered down the tracks,
it will be gone
    just like a child.

By the years
    in which she grows
into another name,
    the toys that we play with
are discarded
    with the commerce of our days.

We'll have shipped the weight
    of innocence and debt
to our cities back home
    and left the tariff hanging
on an empty car
    full of dreamers,
past due bills
    and starlight for direction.

Locomotives whistle.
    We cannot help but dance.

GRILLED CHEESE

James Silas Rogers

One afternoon, making grilled
cheese sandwiches for my daughters,
Margaret declared mine the best in the world.

I demurred. *You might be premature,*
I said. *This is no great art: it's a big
world, with a lot of sandwiches.*

We both smiled. And as I looked
at the breadboard heaped
with cheddar shards, I knew that I had not

always been fully vegetable literate
and, at her age, she could not have thought
that pile looked a lot like rutabagas.

I try never to patronize a child.

EARLY SPRING GARDENING

Larry Smith

Two sisters walk through my yard
whispering around boys' names.
One girl smiles through leaves
the other's arms are pink from sunning,
her blond hair falls on their bareness
like a gown.

Inside the house my own daughter
calls to her sleeping brother.
At thirteen she is all ages,
hair bobbing at her eyes
heart blooming with secrets.
And I think of her mother
home soon from work
dressed in white linen suit
driving her own car now.
Fair sisters, wives, and mothers,
and sweet in their knowing.

The wind blows over me here
turning my hair like leaves
at my collar.
I put seeds into the wet earth
think how nature is all at once forever
how all women are sisters and lovers.

I rise to fix our supper.

STILL CAN'T DO MY
DAUGHTER'S HAIR

WILLIAM EVANS

It is as shameful as it is a relief. I don't know
how to make her more. I reach for her and don't know
how to dull my edges. I fear her scalp
will know I'm a fraud. Will declare my trespass, search
for water and find me the shipwreck.
I clutch her like a blessing I once stole. My blood is
a graceless dancer. My hands are petty prayers. Hold her
like a clumsy ponytail. Like the curtain holds
the wind and its violent song.

I fear that I am not enough. That I am water,
but not enough. I fear the drowning. What I will find
among the ocean floor. My daughter loves me
and a crow is released from my throat. My daughter misses
    me and I
am not worthy. I am not here. Some nights, I kiss her
    goodnight and my jaw unhinges.
Some nights I tuck her in and my fingers become ash.

I leave the house and her voice changes in my head.
It surprises me when I hear it in person. I am boarding
a plane that does not lead back to her. I enter a city where
    she has
never drawn a breath. I read a poem, about my daughter
    and a glass falls from the bar.
This is not a metaphor for what I have lost.
I am afraid of the tide.

Someone calls me a good man and my daughter coughs

herself awake. Pull strands of my daughter's
hair from between my teeth.
I have nightmares, where my daughter forgets my face.
Thinks I am the sun and waits for nightfall.

I have nightmares, where my only child is a boy who is just
like me. I
have nightmares about the sky.
How it looms over me like a flood. I am sleeping
and a child cries in the night. I wake up and she is three
years older. I
wake up alone in a limitless ocean.
There is a child crying from the shore. I do not know
if she is crying out for me.
I have forgotten my own name.

DANSE RUSSE

William Carlos Williams

If I when my wife is sleeping
and the baby and Kathleen
are sleeping
and the sun is a flame-white disc
in silken mists
above shining trees,—
if I in my north room
danced naked, grotesquely
before my mirror
waving my shirt round my head
and singing softly to myself:
"I am lonely, lonely.
I was born to be lonely,
I am best so!"
If I admire my arms, my face,
my shoulders, flanks, buttocks
against the yellow drawn shades,—

Who shall say I am not
the happy genius of my household?

POEM

Peter Stein

is a horrible name for a poem.
No one names their dog 'dog', or cat 'feline'.
We want to call things who or what they are
but never know until we ask.
Even then they cannot say
and wait to be assigned
an assortment of vowels.

Ona walk through the woods,
my son names the trees.
I only know them as
Maple, Poplar, Ash.
He greets each one as
Adam, Rose, Sam.
They seem pleased to be
a sound that resonates
inside another being.

Someday the tree he calls Angela
will take on a new name, like
Tinder, or Paper, or Poem,
and the temptation will be
to name the poem what it is,
but 'Tree' is a horrible name for a poem.

TO DAVID, ABOUT HIS EDUCATION

Howard Nemerov

The world is full of mostly invisible things,
And there is no way but putting the mind's eye,
Or its nose, in a book, to find them out,
Things like the square root of Everest
Or how many times Byron goes into Texas,
Or whether the law of the excluded middle
Applies west of the Rockies. For these
And the like reasons, you have to go to school
And study books and listen to what you are told,
And sometimes try to remember. Though I don't know
What you will do with the mean annual rainfall
On Plato's Republic, or the calorie content
Of the Diet of Worms, such things are said to be
Good for you, and you will have to learn them
In order to become one of the grown-ups
Who sees invisible things neither steadily nor whole,
But keeps gravely the grand confusion of the world
Under his hat, which is where it belongs,
And teaches small children to do this in their turn.

TELL ME WHICH ONE I AM

Alex Lemon

Each day, my child grows
Bigger & I watch him
Like an X-ray, ready to
Excise from his body any
Shadowy growth that
Might make him a magnet
For tragedy –
While each morning
What's up with your face, I ask
The man I stare at in
The mirror. *How is it*
That I know you, again?
I have seen brambles
Of cherry-black clouds
Boiling inside me. I have
Seen myself thigh-deep in
The ocean, confessing
Every cruelty inside me,
Not wanting ever to return
From the salty froth.
Now, my four-year-old boy
Refuses to sleep, says that
After turning five he will
Big enough to close
His eyes. He yawns.
OK, Dada? he mumbles. *Then*
I will close them. When I am
Five. A minute later
He is out – his shut eyes
Blistering with dreams.

I wake on & off & all night,
Finally slip into his room.
I inch my face close enough
To kiss him – until I can be
Sure he's breathing. The turtle
Nightlight beside his bed sprawls
The ceiling with a shining
Midnight. Beneath the slivered
Moon, the scatter of green
Glow-in-the-dark stars, I lay
On the carpet. Closer & closer –
I feel each day that passes
Now. Every breath of mine
Dust-thick, more shallow.
But here, beside him, I will
Last forever—the webbed-

Black dome of night
Pressing down, igniting
All the tiny gods inside me.

PERSEID METEOR SHOWER, 2015

Peter Stein

I want to see the pieces sizzle
before they impact the earth,

but here, even light is pollution.
Two hundred miles and twenty-two years apart

my son camps where it is so dark
he can see everything.

In the morning, he forages
for fragments of sky

ONE SATURDAY MORNING

SEAN HILL

It was spring in Caramel. There were birds. It always
feels like spring in Caramel. It still felt like dep winter
back home in Fairbanks. There were Bushtits and Band-tailed
Pigeons, Acorn Woodpeckers, Western Scrub-Jays
and a Brown Creeper, Black Phoebes, Spotted and California
Towhees, a Townsend's Warbler, and others; a gull floated
high overhead. I stood on the patio in the least layers
I'd worn in months. I held you, legs wrapped by my right arm,
between my wrist and elbow your seat. You'd only recently begun
pointing out the living room window at trucks and cars moving
  along
the hardpack snow on the road back home. There were birds –
a whole new community for you--, and the American Crow
on the wire was the largest, and so I thought the easiest
for your young eyes to perceive, so I pointed up at it, and you
pointed with me with what was surely my hand when
I was your age, but your eyes didn't follow our fingers.
They looked to me and out and inward like when we
listened to music in the kitchen back home in Fairbanks
with our waving hands in the air, but on the patio there
was no music save birdsong. I pulled my hand back
and jabbed it at the crow, and we're doing an old disco move.
I leaned back with you in my arm and watched your eyes
roll down in your head to stay level to the horizon.
After a couple of tries the crow cawed and ruffled its feathers
at us, and you discovered it. O, your emphatic finger showing me
that there was a crow on the wire – acknowledging that bird
and then others. You revealed not what I knew – that there
were birds one Saturday morning in Carmel – but made me feel
again how the world opens before a curious body – our bodies.

STILL LIFE WITH BIRTHDAY CAKE & DYNAMITE

ALEX LEMON

I was alive when this started,
But now, well, who knows

What you'd call this pretty
Little place now? Even after all

That E-coli, I've still got one
Leg that kicks. I've never been

To Waco. I've never been
To Baton Rouge. But I've lived

In an apartment where something
The realtor wouldn't speak

About happened. It was amazing,
How life was altered as I sat

In the living room eating a bowl
Of rice, imagining what kind

Butchery happened – the stained
Hardwood beneath my coffee

Table. Just like today's clouds.
Plumes of acrid smoke are

Wafting above the city & somehow,

I woke with good vibes, thinking
Today was still going to be
A good day. All of the ghosts

Were creep-crawling around
The sugar bowl, right where

I can keep an eye on them.
& that rusty spoon, that bent

Up piece of scrap? Hold the warm
Metal to your lips, my little man.

It's been burning, buried
In my chest for years.

MIMESIS

FADY JOUDAH

My daughter
             wouldn't hurt a spider
That had nested
Between her bicycle handles
For two weeks
She waited
Until it left on its own accord

If you tear down the web I said
It will simply know
This isn't a place to call home
And you'd get to go biking

She said that's how others
Become refugees isn't it?

LULLABY

LI-YOUNG LEE

After crying, Child,
there's still singing to be done.

Your voice, the size of the heart's
first abandonment,
is for naming

the span each falling thing endures,
and then for sounding
a country under speech, dark hillsides

of an older patience outwaiting
what you or your mother and father
could ever say.

What does day proclaim there
where birds glean all of our
remaindered sleep? After wings

and the shadows of wings, there's still
the whole ungrasped body
of flying to uncover.

After standing, outnumbered, under petals
and their raceless falling
out of yesterday
into open want,

we're still the fruit to meet,
still the ancient shapes
of jars and bowls to weigh,

and still the empty hands
in which the hours never pool.

BOUNDLESS

ALEX LEMON

Let's go my little paradise,
My little heart attack –

The city is unwinding.
Roots are busting through

Concrete. Soon, it will no
Longer be the epoch of racing

In circles. There'll be no more
Sleeping in the Xerox machine.

All those disposable hours
Where we sat around wondering

How many times you could
Tell someone that you loved

Them before they'd explode
Instead of leaning into

Their warmth & actually saying
It. Soon, no one will want unlimited

Texts because it will be known –
This here right now, this,

Exactly what you mean –
Is brought to you by

Every second that happens
Hereafter & how the sunrise

Holds your closed eyes.
Any time is the best time

For us to go. Please, hold my hand.
It is such a pleasure to be

Not-dead & walking through
This place with you.

GARY YOUNG

My son put a sheet of paper in the middle of a field to
catch whatever fell from the sky. My son was patient,
not afraid to wait. Under a microscope, he identified
pollen, dead skin, bits of insect wing, and put a magnet
to the rest. He lifted the tiny specks for me to see. he
was old enough to know what he was hungry for, and
what he'd found. Look, he said, stardust.

CLIMBING UP MOUNT VISION
WITH MY LITTLE BOY

Robert Bly

for Noah

We started up. All the way he held my hand. Sometimes
he falls back to bend over a banana slug, then senses how
lonely the slug is, and comes running back. He never
complained, and we went straight up. How much I love
being with him! How much I love to feel his small leafy
hand curl around my finger. He holds on, and we are flying
through a cloud. On top we hunker down beneath some
bushes to get out of the wind, while the girls go off to play,
and he tells me the story of the little boy who wouldn't cut
off his hair and give it to a witch, and so she changed him
into a hollow log. A boy and girl came along, and stepped
on the log – and the log said, "Oww!" They put their feet
on it again, and the log said, "Oww!" Then they looked
inside and saw a boy's jacket sticking out. A little boy was
in there! "I can't come out, I've been changed into a hollow
log." That's the end, he said.

Then I remembered a bit more – the boy and the girl
went to a wise man. . .he corrected me, "It was a wise
woman, Daddy," . . .and said, "How can we get him
changed back into a little boy?" She said, "Here is a pearl. If
a crow asks you for it, give it to him." So they went along.
Pretty soon a crow came and said, "Can I have the buttons
on your shirt?" The boy said, "Yes." Then the crow said,
"Can I have that pearl in your shirt pocket?" "Yes." Then
the crow flew up and dropped some moss down the witch's
chimney. The chimney got full, the witch started to cough.
The crow dropped in some more moss. Then the witch had
to open the door, and run outside! Then the crow took an
oyster, a big one, from the Johnson Oyster Company, and

flew high into the air, and dropped it right on the witch's head. And that was the end of her. And then the boy was changed back again into a little boy.

"That's the end," he said.

STUDENT DRIVER, WAITING TO ENTER TRAFFIC

James Silas Rogers

As soon as she sits down
my daughter twists the radio dial,
and, thinking it my job to scold,
I bark too quickly and too harsh:
Leave the radio alone
for once. She balks but yields
to her place as a student.

She adjusts her seat, draws
so near the wheel she looks
like a moth on a stickpin,
then aligns the side mirrors.
tilts the rearview to her height,
crafting a net of reflection
with herself at the hub.

Driving teaches her the later
uses of mirrors. Hereafter
they point behind her and away;
let her peer into deepening
wells of risk yet hold it afar.
The passing cars clip by
like windmill blades.

WHISKEY WITH MY KIDS

Danny Klecko

Four days after America celebrated its birthday
I celebrated mine
With a number of candles on the cake
That signified this was a day to pay respect
To a man who wasn't over the hill
But could smell the grass on the other side
After eating pasta
After opening gifts
After my wife whisked the grandchildren back home
The evening cooled and somebody suggested
Let's go to Dixie's and drink whiskey with the old man
Hours later, everybody at our table is drunk
It occurs to me, for the first time, my kids are talking to
      each other
Not because they have to, but because they want to
This brought me joy as the server brought the tab
Containing a sum equivalent to a monthly car payment
Cautiously, my kids reach for wallets and purses
Wondering whose responsibility it will be to pay
Somehow protocol is determined in a series of silent glances
That encourages their hands to return to the table
Knowing that the greatest gift they could give their father
Is to let him pay while he is able

SON

TIM NOLAN

Except when he sleeps, I never
get to see the crown of his head.
He always wears a baseball cap.

His jeans hang low off his hips.
This is the fashion. He holds
his hands – as I do – as all the men

in our family hold their hands – shyly.
He's a beautiful boy – smart.
The two of us – we cannot say this

directly – we can only indirectly
acknowledge how beautiful and smart
we are through our mutual

admiration society where we speak
in nods and grunts and mumbles
from the crowns of our beautiful heads.

PHOTOCOPY OF MY DAUGHTER'S FACE

RICHARD BRODERICK

Young girl, trapped beneath the ice,
what are you trying to tell?
That life is a cold, deep well,
a series of gray tones
falling off suddenly to black?

This distortion makes the living
look and shiver.
How long must you wait, child,
face pressed against the light?
In what world will you wake up
and take your next breath?

FATHER'S SONG

GREGORY ORR

Yesterday, against admonishment,
my daughter balanced on the couch back,
fell and cut her mouth.

Because I saw it happen I knew
she was not hurt, and yet
a child's blood so red
it stops a father's heart.

My daughter cried her tears;
I held some ice
against her lip.
That was the end of it.

Round and round: bow and kiss.
I try to teach her caution;
she tries to teach me risk.

BACKYARD BASEBALL

Tim Nolan

Three white plastic chairs
are first, second and third.
My empty wallet is home plate.
Frankie waits patiently on first.

His legs dangle from the chair.
He grows as he waits.
Maeve chokes up on the bulbous
green bat. She is sly beyond

her years. She giggles as I pitch.
Of course it's a hit.
First and second. No outs.
Elizabeth eyes me with suspicion.

She would believe in Santa Claus
if it made enough sense.
Fat and wobbly pitch.
Dished right over the plate.

She tries too hard to hit.
Spins herself around.
Makes herself fall, laughing.
Now she resets. Waits

Definite single to me.
I can't run them down.
Why would I? *Let it be
An endless inning.*

Stranded at their corners.
The sky remains blue—that blue
form the roof of heaven
where we've arrived.

LULLABY FOR A DAUGHTER

JIM HARRISON

Go to sleep. Night is a coal pit
full of black water –
      night's a dark cloud
full of warm rain.

Go to sleep. Night is a flower
resting from bees –
      night's a green sea
swollen with fish.

Got to sleep. Night is a white moon
riding her mare –
      night's a bright sun
burned to black cinder.

Go to sleep
night's come,
cat's day,
owl's day,
star's feast of praise,
moon to reign over
her sweet subject, dark.

GIVE HER THE RIVER

Michael Dennis Browne

If I could give her anything,
  anything at all
in all of the world
  to show how I love her,
I'd give her the river.

Give her the river at dawn,
  when it shines,
when the swans are gliding.

Give her the way the willows
  lean,
how they sway
  in the green of their dreams.

Give her the swallows
  that flicker flicker flicker
over the river of their home.

Give her the old stone steps
  leading down to the river
and the little blue wildflowers
  that are starting to grow there.

Give her the fresh shiny leaves
  of the oaks and elms,
make her a May basket
  from their fluttery shadows.

Give her that line of geese
  headed upstream;
they're honking so hard
  I think they think
they're pulling that boat
  behind them.

Give her the way
  the soft deep water slides
like sleepy us sometimes
  after reading and reading.

Give her that small wooden bench
  where we can sit and watch
the river do all the work
  for a while.

Give her the tinkle of the bell
  on that Scottie's collar
and the grin of the Scottie's owner
  as they jog by.

Give her that one white cloud
  in all the blue sky –
my girl will find some game
  to play with it.

Give her the river at evening,
  we'll smile
at the first of her stars.

Give her the heron
  floating over alone,
and the moon,
  Queen of Herons,
behind her.

Give her the quiet canoe
  that gleams
like a piece of moon.

Give her her very own
  dream of the river
where she sails with friends
  all summer
till she comes to the sea.

Give her the last of the light,
  silvery, silvery,
little waves, little leaves
  little scales, little gleams.

Her river.

FOR MY SON NOAH, TEN YEARS OLD

Robert Bly

Night and day arrive, and day after day goes by,
and what is old remains old, and what is young
      remains young, and grows old.
The lumber pile does not grow younger, nor the
      two-by-fours lose their darkness,
but the old tree goes on, the barn stands without help
      so many years;
the advocate of darkness and night is not lost.

The horse steps up, swings on one leg, turns its body,
the chicken flapping claws onto the roost, its wings
      whelping and walloping,
but what is primitive is not to be shot out into the
      night and the dark.
And slowly the kind man comes closer, loses his rage,
      sits down at table.

So I am proud only of those days that pass in
      undivided tenderness,
when you sit drawing, or making books, stapled,
      with messages to the world,
or coloring a man with fire coming out of his hair.
Or we sit at a table, with small tea carefully poured.
So we pass our time together, calm and delighted.

FLYING DUMBOS

MIKE FINLEY

Taking down my office before the move,
I come across a picture of my daughter and me
at Disneyland, when she was little.
Frozen in the plastic elephant, our faces a riot
of idiot joy, we float high above the pavement
between two other elephants. She is almost three,
and a veteran of seventy screenings of the movie.
Each time she sat reverently through it,
the tension building inside her soft body,
until her eyes open wider than the baby elephant's
and she cries out to the TV, mummo fie, mummo fie,
and looks at me pleadingly so that I too can affirm
the miracle of flesh borne aloft with neither net
nor magic feather, and I take her pudgy hands in mine
and clap them for her.

TOURIST WITH DAUGHTER

Bao Phi

I sit with our daughter at the top of the Space Needle
eating hot dogs we paid tourist prices for.
It's fine, really, in this place high up, these assumptions
of who we are and what we can afford.

I want to tell our daughter that my dad could never afford
Something like this for me.
But what good would that be.

I'm not using her name in this poem because
she hasn't given me permission.

When I was about six, my dad looked me in the eye
and challenged me to point out one time
he failed to keep me a promise.
I thought then of half a dozen occasions but stayed silent.

I ask our daughter what she likes up here and she says
the clouds, and the boats.

From up this high you think you can see everything.
I'm amazed she likes sour corn syrup sticky candy more than a
Kobe beef hot dog.

When she looks bored, I want to tell her that
we can't always have what we want.
When really, some us can never have what we want.

But instead I stay silent,
look at the clouds and the boats
as if for the first time.

ARS POETICA

MICHAEL KLEBER-DIGGS

Last night in my dream
I wanted something ordinary –
sugar or a hammer, something
like that, so I asked a neighbor,

but not an actual neighbor.
I rang a doorbell. Behind the door,
a man yelled "I've called the police"
(I'm black even in my dreams).

"Ok," I said. "Do you mind
if I wait here for them?"
He must have said "no"
'cause I sat on his front steps.

At some point, he appeared
next to me; we talked
but shared no kept words.
We were calm, chatting –

our alarms quieted – unafraid.
I woke up before the officers arrived,
but not on purpose.
I usually wake into darkness –

my dreams gone, lost, beyond
my reach, my cortex – into ether.
Or maybe that's what I tell myself'
it's possible I practice forgetting.

I'm writing this on my phone
while I teach my daughter to drive.
I should pay attention more than I do,
but she is managing well. I don't want

to lose this idea. "I'm working on a poem,"
I tell her. "What about?" she asks.
I say. "That's cool," she answers.
I add "I don't usually remember

my dreams. I think I want more
from them – like magic, something
fantastic. Maybe I could breathe
underwater, or be miniscule or grow

an epic beard, or maybe all three
at the same time. But, of course,
my vision would be ordinary,
some thing that could actually happen."

My daughter sits like a dancer,
tall and open. Her hands are powerful
and light. In them the steering
wheel becomes a ballet barre.

She's focused, but almost somewhere
else, like we're in her studio.
"I always remember mine," she says.
"They're strange. Once I dreamed

I pooped out a yellow snake
then became friends with it..."
"Are you shitting me?" I ask her.
I know I'm wrong to envy, to want.

And why must I act silly
before I confess something
serious? – I say "You are
the kind of artist I want to be."

She keeps her eyes on the road.
She makes the window a mirror,
and meets me there instead.
She knows I'm taking this down –

all of it.

THE WRITER

RICHARD WILBUR

In her room at the prow of the house
Where light breaks, and the windows are tossed with linden,
My daughter is writing a story.

I pause in the stairwell, hearing
From here shut door a commotion of typewriter-keys.
Like a chain hauled over a gunwale.

Young as she is, the stuff
Of her life is a great cargo, and some of it heavy:
I wish her a lucky passage.

But now it is she who pauses,
As if to reject my thought and its easy figure.
A stillness greatens, in which

The whole house seems to be thinking,
And then she is at it again with a bunched clamor
Of strokes, and again is silent.

I remember the dazed starling
Which was trapped in that very room, two years ago;
How we stole in, lifted a sash

And retreated, not to affright it;
And how for a helpless hour, through the crack of the door,
We watched the sleek, wild, dark

And iridescent creature
Batter against the brilliance, drop like a glove
To the hard floor, or the desk-top,

And wait then, humped and bloody,
For the wits to try it again; and how our spirits
Rose when, suddenly sure,

It lifted off from a chair-back,
Beating a smooth course for the right window
And clearing the sill of the world.

It is always a matter, my darling,
Of life or death, as I had forgotten. I wish
What I wished you before, but harder.

DRESSING MY DAUGHTERS

MARK JARMAN

One girl a full head taller
Than the other – into their Sunday dresses.
First, the slip, hardly a piece of fabric,
Softly stitched and printed with a bud.
I'm not their mother, and tangle, then untangle
The whole cloth—on backwards, have to grab it
Round their necks. But they know how to pull
Arms in, a reflex of being dressed,
And also, a child's faith. The mass of stuff
That makes the Sunday frocks collapses
In my hands and finds its shape, only because
They understand the drape of it—
These skinny keys to intricate locks.
The buttons are a problem
For a surgeon. How would she connect
These bony valves and stubborn eyelets?
The filmy dress revolves in my blind fingers.
The slots work one by one.
And when they're put together,
Not like puppets or those doll-saints
That bring tears to true believers,
But living children, somebody's real daughters,
They do become more real.
They say, "Stop it!" and "Give it back!"
And " I don't want to!" They'll kiss
A doll's hard features, whispering,
"I'm sorry." I know just why my mother
Used to worry. Your clothes don't keep
You close—it's nakedness.
Clad in my boots and holster,

I would roam with my six-gun buddies.
We dealt fake death to one another,
Fell and rolled in filth and rose,
Grimy with wounds, then headed home.
But Sunday ... what was that tired explanation
Given for wearing clothes that
Scratched and shone and weighed like a slow hour?
That we should shine—in gratitude.
So, I give that explanation, undressing them,
And wait for the result.
After a day like Sunday, such a long one,
When they lie down, half-dead,
To be undone, they won't help me.
They cry, "It's not my fault."

SNOW

Seido Ray Ronci

On my way out the door, my son says,
"Dad, I have to poop."
After all the work of bundling him up,
"Go ahead," I say.
He sheds his parka, drops his snow pants,
and mounts the high white seat of the toilet.
I unbutton my coat, loosen my scarf,
let it hang form my neck, and wait.
Almost immediately he calls from the bathroom:
"Papa, check my bottom."
I lean over the small of his back as he bows,
lost in the flurry of my overcoat and scarf.
I wipe the crack of his ass. He hops off
the toilet and pulls up his pants, I flush,
and see shit on the fringe of my scarf;
disbelieving, I hold it up to the light,
"There's shit on my scarf!"
He puts on his coat, mittens and hat.
I'm reminded of the young monk Ikkyu
wiping Kaso's shriveled ass with his bare hands,
washing his master's frail body, rinsing
the soiled sheets, wringing them out
day and night till the old man's death.
I think, too, of the stains on my father's bed,
the nurses drawing the curtains to clean him,
his sunken eyes, looking into mine, ashamed.
"It's alright, Dad," I say.
"It's not all right," he says.
My son tromps to the door, flings it open;
a blast of cold air rushes through the house.

I wash the fringe in the sink, tighten
my scarf and raise my collar.
He's making angels in the snow.

WITH KIT, AGE 7, AT THE BEACH

William Stafford

We would climb the highest dune,
from there to gaze and come down:
the ocean was performing;
we continued our climb.

Waves leapfrogged and came
straight out of the storm.
What should our gaze mean?
Kit waited for me to decide.

Standing on such a hill,
what would you tell your child?
That was an absolute vista.
Those waves raced far, and cold.

'How far could you swim, Daddy,
in such a storm?'
'As far as was needed,' I said,
and as I talked, I swam.

TEACHING HER TO DRIVE

Mike Finley

Because she was phobic, it took us six years.
She was afraid of oncoming cars,
so afraid she put her hands up when they passed.
I had to find places where she felt safe,
so I chose cemetery roads,
with their strange curves,
and mourners making their way back to their cars,
white Kleenex against black clothing.
We graduated to suburban lanes, practicing every Saturday,
month after month, until I let her drive us back into the
      city
the length of South Lyndale Avenue.
Three times she failed her exam,
and each time I encouraged her.
Everyone fails a couple of times, I said.
You'll get it, don't worry.
But I was shaking the fourth time out,
exiting the car and fretting over how she would take
a fourth failure.
After the exam she sat in the car with the instructor
for what seemed like an hour.
When she stepped out, she walked across the blacktop
toward me, a grin slowly forming on her face,
and I broke down blubbering,
tears running into my mouth, thinking,
This will change everything.

THREE

Another word for father is worry.

-Li-Young Lee

FRACTALS

RICHARD BRODERICK

Your son looks at the frost
on a café window and tells you
he would like to capture its image,
this structure and form that's
crazed but perfectly realized.
Its fractals, explains this young man
interested in art and physics
and the depths of the unknown.
It's like the coastline
of a barrier island, every section
of it could be stretched out
to form a line encircling the world.
You dip your toast into your eggs
and listen. At times – often –
you fear that he may be lost,
but you console yourself
with this simple thought. After all,
isn't that the cost some must pay
to find their way to shore?

PRAYING HANDS CAN'T CATCH BULLETS

PETER STEIN

I am at a loss at how to talk to my children
about the Paris terror attacks while their school
teaches them how to respond in a lockdown:
"Here is your shield; you can use it to hold books.
This semester you'll be assigned Tolstoy."

I sit them down like a confessor,
"Forgive me, child, for I have sinned,"
and pray for the absolution of the world I brought them into.

In physics they learn bullets don't fly, they fall
    at the same rate as everything else
in this gravity, yet at their velocity
    the force I greater than a contracting heart

Intro to Law defends open carry as the second commandment
but reinforces students will get arrested for shooting their
mouths off.
Religious rights defend the freedom to shoot first
but guardian angels don't wear Kevlar.

My hugs have holes, my arms
don't reach far enough to smother
the guns drawn. Someone fires back
at someone firing back at someone
firing at me for being overprotective.
I have lost faith that God will sort this out.
Yes, there are monsters in your closet.
No, I will not spend the night in your room—

I am afraid of them too.
Now say your prayers
and go to sleep

THE KIDS

Tim Nolan

At work during the day
your old pictures
on my window ledge

Various stages
of the various *yous*
each one of the *yous*

The three of *yous*
Holding signs that say
Happy... Father's... Day

It's one of those moments
that could slay me
if I let it

Your eyes those years ago
remain the same
for each of you

Isn't this *The Iliad*
as well as *The Odyssey*
the heroic past?

It's everything this snapshot
all the king's ransom
all the privileges of the realm

MY DAUGHTER DANCES TO THE MOON

Hardy Coleman

A rose, two-ninety-five at the corner store
     red as flow
red as blood tide at full moon,
     and it earns me a kiss.

And all the kisses that I never got
     when I was twelve
linger in my beard as if to say
     "I am your child. So I am a goddess."

Ah daughter, I'd like to give you secrets
     that were never told to me,
string them on a necklace
     gathered from the sea,
and a thousand things I never knew,
     will never learn, have found forever out of reach …
I'll put them in a hope chest,
     I'll sew them in with ribbons
          on your pretty wedding dress.

This long stem single rose
     is my first goodbye
to you, my little girl.
     Other gifts will follow. Take them. Pass them down.
They are not mine, were not my father's,
     but my grandchildren will wear them
          like this flower in your hair.

And I know, I know that someday
    I will miss you
and another man will take my place.
      But oh, thank you! My child in her rhythm,
        for I will always be
            the very first boy that you ever
            ever kissed.

When your children ask, will you always love me, say
you will love them forever, and then tell them what
forever means. You can explain the heavens if they ask,
and tell them, your bodies are made from the dust
of shattered stars. But when they ask you, will I ever
die, then lie to them. They're still young, and it might
frighten them if you said, no.

THE AMERICAN CENTURY

KENNETH REXROTH

Blackbirds whistle over the young
Willow leaves, pale celadon green,
In the cleft of the emerald hills.
My daughter is twenty-one months old.
Already she knows the names of
Many birds and flowers and all
The animals of the barnyard and zoo.
She paddles in the stream, chasing
Tiny bright green frogs. She wants
To catch them and kiss them. Now she
Runs to me with a tuft of rose
Gray owl's clover. "What's that? Oh! What's that??
She hoots like an owl and caresses
The flower when I tell her its name.
Overhead in the deep sky
Of May Day jet bombers cut long
White slashes of smoke. The blackbird
Sings and the baby laughs, midway
In the century of horror.

LAYERS

James Silas Rogers

for my daughter

Queen Anne's Lace everywhere, the day
we left you and drove back from Illinois.
Along the road to Lincoln, it hung
over all the uncultivated spaces.
between the soybean fields and the shoulders,
like a stratus of morning fog. You deserve
to be remembered by a lovelier flower
than a species of wild carrot spread at random,
nubbly crowns the color of window putty.
Long ago, when you were in your infancy
I told my friend, *I think this is the child*
who will break my heart. How wrong
I was, how wrong. That day in August
I wanted to cry, but cannot be sad
you left for an uncertain Providence;
not even when Queen Anne's Lace seizes the land
like an early snow, when its wan flowers scatter
everywhere, like the residue of a flood.

LETTER OF THE LAW

Hardy Coleman

for Marga

I'd bought us a kite
    painted as a flock of
variegated birds,
    and on it's maiden flight
the string broke and it
    took to the heavens.
You choked up and asked,
    "Where did it go?"

I've had some time
    to consider your question.

Still, I can't give you any maps.
    Just pictures of me
smiling for the camera,
    holding you in my lap.

You're much too big for that now, girl.

And tonight, I set the table, inviting guests
    and neighbors.
Haltingly and they pause and
    check out the wares.
But they do not share my bounty
    and it's cold
outside and I wish
    I weren't all alone and old,
peeling band-aids off the past.
    Yes, your tears
have tethered me to childhood

scrapes and owies.
I will airmail this epistle
        to beg your comfort,
though you don't bring me
        to play in the park these days;
Having you own flock to raise,
        having your own tear stained photographs
to snap
        and flutter away.

JOURNAL FOR MY DAUGHTER

STANLEY KUNITZ

1

Your turn. Grass of confusion.
You say you had a father once:
his name was absence.
He left, but did not let you go.
Part of him, more than a shadow,
beckoned down corridors,
secret, elusive, saturnine,
melting at your touch.
In the crack
of a divided house
grew the resentment-weed.
It has white inconspicuous flowers
Family of anthologists!
Collectors of injuries!

2

I wake to a glittering world,
to the annunciation of the frost.
A popeyed chipmunk scurries past,
the pockets of his cheeks bulging.
As the field mice store seeds,
as the needle-nosed shrew
threading under the woodpile
deposits little heaps of land-snails
for milestones on its runways,
I promise
that we gather our affections.
Lambkin, I care.

3

I was happy you were born,
your banks of digits
equipped for decimals,
and all your clever parts
neatly in place.
Your nation gives me joy,
as it has always given.
If I could have my choice
on the way to exile
I think I'd rather sleep forever
than wake up cold
in a country without women.

4

You cried. You cried.
You wasted and you cried.
Night after night
I walked the floor with you,
croaking the same old
tranquilizing song,
the only tune
I ever learned to carry.
In the rosy tissue
of your brain,
where memory begins,
that theme is surely scored,
waiting till you need
to play it back.
There were three crows
sat on a tree
Sing Billy Magee Magaw.
You do not need to sing to me.
I like the sound of your voice

even when you phone from school
asking for money.

5

There was a big blond uncle-bear,
wounded, smoke-eyed, wild,
who shambled from the west
with his bags full of havoc.
He spoke the bears' grunt-language,
waving his paws
and rocking on his legs.
Both of us were drunk,
slapping each other on the back,
sweaty with genius.
He spouted his nonsense-rhymes,
roaring like a behemoth.
You crawled under the sofa.

6

Goodies are shaken
from the papa-tree:
Be what you are. Give
what is yours to give.
Have style. Dare.
Such a storm of fortune cookies!
Outside your room
stands the white-headed prowler
in his multiple disguises
who reminds you of your likeness.
Wherever you turn,
down whatever street,
in the fugues of appetite,
in the groin of nightmare,
he waits for you,

haggard with his thousand years.
His agents are everywhere,
his heart is at home
in your own generation;
the folded message in his hands
is stiff with dirt and wine-stains,
older than the Dead Sea Scrolls.
Daughter, read:
What do I want of my life?
More! More!

      7

Demonstrations in the streets.
I am there not there,
ever uneasy in a crowd.
But you belong,
flaunting your home-made
insubordinate flag.
Why should I be surprised?
We come of a flinty maverick line.
In my father's time, I'm told,
our table was set in turn
for Maxim Gorky, Emma Goldman,
and the atheist Ingersoll.
If your slogan is misspelt
Don't tred on me!
still it strikes
parents and politicians down.
Noli me tangere! is what
I used to cry in Latin once.
Oh to be radical, young, desirable, cool!

8

Your first dog was a Pekinese,
fat and saucy Ko-San,
half mandarin, half mini-lion,
who chased milkmen and mailmen
and bit the tires of every passing car
till a U.S. Royal bit him back.
You sobbed for half an hour,
then romped to the burial service
in the lower garden
by the ferny creek.
I helped you pick the stones
to mark his shallow grave.
It was the summer I went away.
One night I carried you outdoors,
in a blitz of fireflies,
to watch your first eclipse.
Your far-off voice,
drugged with milk and sleep,
said it was a leaf
sliding over the light.

9

The night when Coleridge,
heavy-hearted,
bore his crying child outside,
he noted
that those brimming eyes
caught the reflection
of the starry sky,
and each suspended tear
made a sparkling moon.

A MEMORIAL: SON BRET

WILLIAM STAFFORD

In the way you went you were important.
I do not know what you found.
In the pattern of my life you stand
where you stood always, in the center,
a hero, a puzzle, a man.

What you might have told me
I will never know—the lips went still,
the body cold. I am afraid,
in the circling, in the dark,
and even at noon in the light.

When I run, what am I running from?
You turned once to tell me something,
but then you glimpsed a shadow on my face
and maybe thought, why tell what hurts?
You carried it, my boy, so brave, so far.

Now we have all the days, and the sun
goes by the same;
there is a faint,
wandering trail I find sometimes, off
through the grass and sage. I stop
and listen, only summer again—remember?—
set off like other strangers

The bees, the wind.

THE SHADBLOW TREE

David Budbill

It's the tenth of May
        and the shadblow tree
we planted to honor
        our son's death—
he died at the age of forty—
        is in full bloom now.

It's a white cloud hovering
        at the edge of the
gardens, just as Gene
        hovers at the edge
of our lives.

WAVING GOOD-BYE

GERALD STERN

I wanted to know what it was like before we
had voices and before we had bare fingers and before we
had minds to move us through our actions
and tears to help us over our feelings,
so I drove my daughter through the snow to meet her friend
and filled her car with suitcases and hugged her
as an animal would, pressing my forehead against her,
walking in circles, moaning, touching her cheek,
and turned my head after them as an animal would,
watching helplessly as they drove over the ruts,
her smiling face and her small hand just visible
over the giant pillows and coat hangers
as they made their turn into the empty highway.

PITTSBURGH

Hayden Carruth

And my beautiful daughter
had her liver cut open in Pittsburgh.
My god, my god! I rubbed
her back over the swollen and wounded
essentiality, I massaged
her legs, and we talked of death.
At the luckiest patients with liver cancer have
a 20% chance. We might have talked
of my death, not long to come. But no,
the falling into death of a beautiful
young woman is so much more important.
A wonderful hospital. If I must die
away from my cat Smudge and my Vermont Castings stove
let it be at Allegheny General.
I read to her, a novella by Allan Gurganus,
a Russian serious of flimsiness by Voinovich,
and we talked. We laughed. We actually
laughed. I brought her a lipstick
which she wore though she disliked the color.
Helicopters took off and landed on the hospital pad,
bringing the hearts and kidneys and maybe livers
from other places to be transplanted
into people in the shining household of technology
by shining technologists, wise and kindly.
The chances are so slight. Oh, my daughter,
my love for you has burgeoned—
an excess of singularity ever increasing—
you are my soul—for forty years. You
still beautiful and young. In my hotel
I could not sleep. In my woods, on my

little farm, in the blizzard on the mountain,
I could not sleep either, but scribbled
fast verses, very fast and
wet with my heartsblood and brainjuice
all my life, as now
in Pittsburgh. I don't know which of
us will live the longer, it's all a flick
of the wrist of the god mankind invented
and then had to deinvent, such a failure, like all
our failures, and the worst and best
is sentimentality after all. Let us go out together.
Here in brutal Pittsburgh. Let us
be together in the same room,
the old poet and the young painter,
holding hands, a calm touch, a whisper,
as the thumping helicopters go out and come in,
we in the crisis of forever inadequately medicated
pain, in the love of daughter and father.

MOLLY IN THE DOOR

Mike Finley

I went to the door and there was my daughter.
The sun was shining behind her
so I could barely make out her face
but I could see she was healthy
and strong and happy.
Hi Pops, she slugged me,
the way she always did,
and she gave me the biggest hug.
She held me in my arms and spun me slowly around,
spun her old man around,
rocking me on my feet.
I was astonished at her musculature
and the bright look in her eye,
it was joyous, and fearless
like she had been paddling a canoe in the sun
with good friends for a year.
I held on and began to cry…
I woke up.
At first I was sad because it wasn't true,
my daughter wasn't really alive.
I would never hold her and swing her like that again.
But then I thought this
is how she might be now,
easy and forgiving and strong as a horse,
and I began to laugh
the same way she used to laugh,
eyes closed, top teeth showing,
like a semi-moon on a starless night,
letting it out in one long exhalation,
holding nothing back.

WINDY FALL

Kobayashi Issa

translated by Robert Hass

At my daughter's grave, thirty days
after her death:

Windy fall—
these are the scarlet flowers
she liked to pick.

FOR MY DAUGHTER IN REPLY TO A QUESTION

DAVID IGNATOW

We're not going to die,
we'll find a way.
We'll breathe deeply
and eat carefully.
We'll think always on life.
There'll be no fading for you or for me.
We'll be the first
and we'll not laugh at ourselves ever
and your children will be my grandchildren.
Nothing will have changed
except by addition.
There'll never be another as you
and never another as I.
No one ever will confuse you
nor confuse me with another.
We will not be forgotten and passed over
and buried under the births and deaths to come.

AUBADE

David Mura

A wound is a blossom
but only to the living.
A May night, birdsong

before the first light pierces,
chirps out of blackness:
My daughter's angry at me

and her mother as I
was once angry at mine.
It's a way of crossing over.

I'm so tired now.
And my core's
all water, flowing

somewhere where the sea
can't find her. And neither
can I. How much longer

till I finally lose her? Where
is the first dawn wet blossom?
Who recalls how I touched

her mother once? Or many others?
How night is not always easy.
Nor are daughters. Nor are sons.

And how is it I've become a father
watching light sift slowly
into the daughterless dark.

LOSING A DAUGHTER IS LIKE BEING A BEE ON THE MOON

Mike Finley

Every morning you wake up shivering
gazing out at the darkened spires,
wondering where is a flower
in this barren land that you
can draw some sweetness from.

FATHER-SON ADVICE AT 50

James P. Lenfestey

He called.   Things
are not good right now.

And how are you?
Sleepless.   Things.

Is there …? What …?
I have so much more …

How smart the children are.
And fathers.
How is it we starve?

The textbook for today
Is written
today. The cookbook says,
sear everything.

LAST WILL AND TESTAMENT

Thomas McGrath

for Tomasito

Son,
Forgive me:
When you were little,
I made some money,
Once,
And saved it
For what they call
Your "future"
And,
Alas,
I did it without
Robbing a bank.

Forgive me, son,
(And all other children) that,
One time,
I made an agreement with
The enemy.

FOR MY DAUGHTER

David Ignatow

When I die choose a star
and name it after me
that you may know
I have not abandoned
or forgotten you.
You were such a star to me,
following you through birth
and childhood, my hand
in your hand.

When I die
choose a star and name it
after me so that I may shine
down on you, until you join
me in darkness and silence
together.

ACKNOWLEDGEMENTS

Yehuda Amichai, "On the Day my Daughter was born no one died" from *The Selected Poems of Yehuda Amichai*, translated by Chana Bloch and Stephen Mitchell. Copyright 2013, reprinted by permission of the University of California Press.

Robert Bly, "For my Son Noah, 10 Years Old" from *The Man in the Black Coat Turns* by Robert Bly. Copyright 1981 by Robert Bly. Reprinted by permission of Georges Borchardt, Inc., for Robert Bly. "Climbing up Mount Vision with my Little Boy" from *Reaching out to the World: New & Selected Prose Poems* by Robert Bly. Copyright 2009 by Robert Bly. Reprinted by permission of White Pine Press.

Philip Booth, "First Lesson" from *Lifelines: Selected Poems 1950-1999* by Philip Booth, copyright 1999 by Philip Booth. Used by permission of Viking Books, an imprint of Penguin Publishing Group, a division of Penguin Random House LLC. All rights reserved.

Richard Broderick, "Photocopy of my Daughter's Face" from *Woman Lake*. Copyright 2000 by Richard Broderick. Reprinted by permission of New Rivers Press. "Fractals" copyright 2018 by Richard Broderick. Reprinted by permission of the author.

Michael Dennis Browne, "Give her the River," from *Give Her the River: A Father's Wish for His Daughter*. Copyright 2004 by Michael Dennis Browne. Reprinted by Permission of Atheneum Books for Young Readers.

David Budbill, "The Shadblow Tree" from *Tumbling Toward the End*. Copyright 2017 by David Budbill. Reprinted with the permission of The Permissions Company, Inc., on behalf of Copper Canyon Press, www.coppercanyonpress.org.

Charles Bukowski, "marina" from *Mockingbird Wish Me Luck*. Copyright 1972 by Charles Bukowski. Reprinted with the permission of Harper Collins Publishing.

Hayden Carruth, "Pittsburgh" from *Scrambled Eggs and Whiskey*. Copyright 1996 by Hayden Carruth. Reprinted with the permission of The Permissions Company, Inc., on behalf of Copper Canyon Press, www.coppercanyonpress.org.

2000 by Richard Jones. Reprinted with the permission of The Permissions Company, Inc., on behalf of Copper Canyon Press, www.coppercanyonpress.org.

Fady Joudah, "Minesis" from *Alight*. Copyright 2013 by Fady Joudah. Reprinted with the permission of The Permissions Company, Inc., on behalf of Copper Canyon Press, www.coppercanyonpress.org.

Danny Klecko, "Whiskey with my Kids" from *Brando Land*. Copyright 2017 by Danny Klecko. Reprinted by permission of Kraken Press.

Stanley Kunitz, "Journal for my Daughter" from *The Collected Poems* by Stanley Kunitz. Copyright 2000 by Stanley Kunitz. Used by permission of W.W. Norton & Company, Inc.

Li-Young Lee, "Lullaby" from *Book of My Nights*. Copyright 2001 by Li-Young Lee. Reprinted with the permission of The Permissions Company, Inc., on behalf of BOA Editions, Ltd., www.boaeditions.org.

Alex Lemon, "I Knew You Before You Were," "Boundless," and "Still Life with Birthday Cake & Dynamite" from *The Wish Book* by Alex Lemon (Minneapolis: Milkweed Editions, 2014). Copyright 2014 by Alex Lemon. Reprinted with permission from Milkweed Editions. www.milkweed.org. "Tell me Which One I Am" copyright 2018 by Alex Lemon. Reprinted with permission of the author.

James Lenfestey, "To Make a Baby," from *Family Matters: Poems of our Families*, edited by Ann Smith and Larry Smith. Copyright 2005 by James Lenfestey. Reprinted with permission of Bottom Dog Press. "Father-Son Advice at 50" copyright 2018 by James Lenfestey, used by permission of the author.

Thomas McGrath, "Last Will and Testament" from *Death Song*. Copyright 1991 by Thomas McGrath. Reprinted with the permission of The Permissions Company, Inc., on behalf of Copper Canyon Press, www.coppercanyonpress.org.

David Mura, "Aubade" from "Things that Lose by Being Painted (a fiction)" in *The Last Incantations: Poems*. Copyright 2014 by David Mura. Reprinted by permission of TriQuarterly Books/Northwestern University Press.

Howard Nmerov, "September, the First Day of School" and "To David, About His Education" from *Trying Conclusions: New and Selected Poems 1961-1991* (University of Chicago Press). Used by permission of the Estate of Howard Nemerov.

Greg Watson's work has appeared in numerous literary journals and anthologies, including *The Wind Blows, the Ice Breaks: Poems of Loss and Renewal by Minnesota Poets*, and the *Saint Paul Almanac*. His most recent collection is *All the World at Once: New and Selected Poems*, published by Nodin Press.

Richard Broderick is the author of three books of poetry, including *Jesus of Walmart*, and a collection of short fiction. Recipient of numerous grants, he is the co-editor of *Great River Review*.